MARTIAL ARTS LEGENDS

Clive Gifford

Copyright © ticktock Entertainment Ltd 2009

First published in Great Britain in 2009 by ticktock Media Ltd,
The Old Sawmill, 103 Goods Station Road, Tunbridge Wells, Kent, TN1 2DP

project editor and picture researcher: Ruth Owen
ticktock project designer: Simon Fenn

With thanks to Dave Hazard and Bernard Rose, and Bill Wallace and Rob (Mr. V) Vanelli.

Thank you to Lorraine Petersen and the members of nasen

ISBN 978 1 84696 940 9 pbk

Printed in China

Picture credits (t=top; b=bottom; c=centre; l=left; r=right):
AFP/Getty Images: 16, 20-21, 28. David Appleby/Buena Vista Pictures/Bureau L.A. Collection/Corbis: OFC. Bernard
Rose Photography: p9 (all). Everett Collection/Rex Features: 10-11, 19. Game of Death Concord Productions/RGA: 15.
Getty Images: 17, 29tl. Gichin Funakoshi public domain: 8. Kodokan: 7t. Miramax/Everett/Rex Features: 18. Bazuki
MuhammadA/Reuters/Corbis: 6. Popperfoto/Getty Images: 7b. Redchopsticks.com LLC/Alamy: 7c. Rocky IV Chartoff
Winkler Productions/RGA: 14. Drew Serrano, East Coast Training Systems: 22-23. Shutterstock: 1, 2, 4-5, 8-9
(background), 14-15 (background), 16-17 (background), 24-25 (main), 26-27, 27r (all), 29t, 31. John Springer
Collection/Corbis: 12-13. Morihei Ueshiba public domain: 24 (inset), 25r (all).

Every effort has been made to trace copyright holders, and we apologise in advance for any omissions. We would be pleased to
insert the appropriate acknowledgments in any subsequent edition of this publication.

CONTENTS

MARTIAL ARTS

Martial arts were developed to be used in battle.

Most martial arts are types of hand-to-hand fighting without weapons.

Some martial arts are over 3,000 years old. Many were developed in Asia.

Judo

Some, such as judo, use holds and throws.

Others, such as karate and kickboxing, use strikes of the foot and hand.

Each martial art has different styles or schools. The Chinese martial art of Kung Fu has over 400 different schools.

Today, martial arts are used for self-defence, exercise and as sports.

Karate

MARTIAL ARTS TIMELINE

Here are some important events in the history of martial arts.

Shaolin monks develop martial arts
Around 1500 years ago, the first Shaolin monk temple was built in China. The monks began to develop many different martial arts.

Chinese Shaolin Kung Fu monks

The invention of judo

In 1882, judo was invented by a Japanese man named Jigoro Kano. In 1909, Kano became the first Asian member of the International Olympic Committee.

Jigoro Kano

Martial arts safety

Jhoon Rhee is a taekwondo master. He moved from Korea to America in 1956. In the 1970s, he invented padded safety kit.

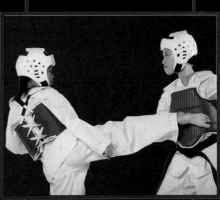

Kickboxers in safety kit

Olympic judo

Judo first appeared at the Olympics in 1964. Anton Geesink was the only gold medallist not from Japan. His success helped make judo more popular around the world.

1964 - Anton Geesink in action

Olympic taekwondo

In 2000, taekwondo became an Olympic sport.

GICHIN FUNAKOSHI

Karate began many centuries ago on a tiny group of islands off the coast of Japan.

People were banned by their leaders from carrying weapons. They developed martial arts instead.

Gichin Funakoshi was born on the Okinawa Islands, off Japan, in 1868. Funakoshi practised karate.

In 1917, Funakoshi took karate to mainland Japan.

In 1936, Funakoshi built the first karate school in Japan. He founded Shotokan karate – the most popular karate style.

Funakoshi's students took karate to Europe and America. Funakoshi is the man most responsible for the spread of karate around the world.

Side thrust kick

Rooted stance with high and low defence

Here, Shotokan instructor Dave Hazard demonstrates some stances and moves.

Horse stance with lower defence

Cat stance with chicken wrist block

BRUCE LEE'S STORY

Bruce Lee was the star of martial arts movies such as _Enter the Dragon_ and _Fists of Fury._

Lee's martial arts moves were amazingly fast.

Movie-makers had to use slow motion cameras so people could see his moves.

In 1973, Lee died suddenly.
He was just 32 years old and very fit.

There are lots of ideas about why Bruce Lee died.
- A bad reaction to headache tablets.
- He was murdered by a Hong Kong Triad gang.
- A family curse – his son, Brandon Lee, died 20 years later.
- He was killed by a "death touch strike" from a jealous martial artist.

Lee developed his own martial art. It is called Jeet Kune Do. It means "the way of the intercepting fist".

A TRUE LEGEND

Bruce Lee could:

- Make a 3 centimetre punch which knocked a 100 kilogram man back 5 metres.

- Perform one-handed push-ups using just one finger and thumb.

- Pierce an unopened steel soft drinks can using just his fingers.

MOVIE MAGIC

Many action movie stars are martial arts legends. Here are two of the best!

Dolph Lundgren
- Height: 1.96 m
- Country: Sweden

Won the European Karate Championships heavyweight title in 1980 and 1981.

Lundgren has appeared in over 35 movies.

Dolph Lundgren (right) and Sylvester Stallone in the movie, Rocky IV.

Chuck Norris

- Height: 1.78 m
- Country: USA

Norris was the Professional World Middleweight Karate Champion. He was undefeated for six years until he retired in 1974.

Norris starred in movies and taught martial arts to other Hollywood stars.

Chuck Norris with Bruce Lee in the movie, Game of Death.

STEVEN LOPEZ

Taekwondo comes from Korea. Taekwondo means "the way of the foot and fist".

The first Olympic gold medal in taekwondo went to an American, Steven Lopez, in 2000.

Lopez followed it up with a second Olympic gold in 2004.

Steven Lopez (in red) at the Beijing Olympics, 2008

Lopez comes from an amazing taekwondo family.

The Lopez brothers and sister all appeared at the 2008 Olympics.

Steven Lopez
bronze medallist

Diana Lopez
bronze medallist

Jean Lopez
US team coach

Mark Lopez
silver medallist

JACKIE CHAN

Jackie Chan joined the China Drama Academy when he was just seven.

At the academy, Chan learned acrobatics, weapons training and acting. He also learned wushu. This is a type of martial art that was invented in China in the 20th century.

Chan's martial arts training helped him perform hundreds of amazing stunts in his movies.

Chan's daredevil stunts have led to many injuries.

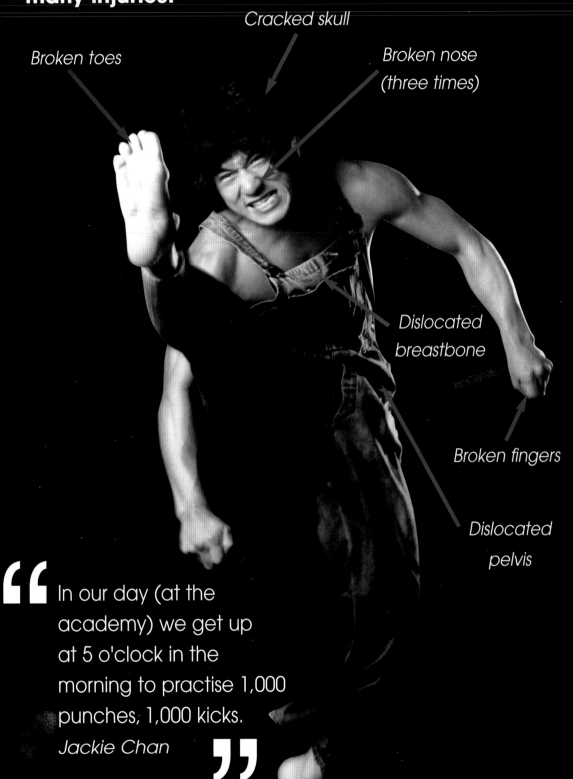

Cracked skull

Broken toes

Broken nose
(three times)

Dislocated
breastbone

Broken fingers

Dislocated
pelvis

" In our day (at the academy) we get up at 5 o'clock in the morning to practise 1,000 punches, 1,000 kicks.
Jackie Chan "

RYOKO TANI

Ryoko Tani is only 1.46 metres tall. She weighs less than 48 kilograms. Yet, she is the most famous and feared female judoka of all.

Why?

Tani has competed in five Olympic Games. She has won a medal every time.

Tani was just 16 when she won silver at the 1992 Olympics.

In the final of the 2000 Olympics, Tani took just 40 seconds to win gold.

From 1993 to 1996, Tani was unbeaten in an amazing 84 judo bouts.

2004 – Athens Olympics final

Ryoko Tani (Japan)

Frederique Jossinet (France)

RECORD BREAKERS

Some martial artists practise their striking moves on wooden boards and concrete blocks. This has led to some smashing records!

Martial arts expert Drew Serrano makes a perfect "drop elbow" through a stack of concrete blocks

Fernando Camareno
468 concrete tiles in one minute
(2007)

Muhamed Kahrimanovic
81 coconuts in one minute
(2007)

Leif Becker
487 wooden boards in one minute
(2005)

Larry Fields
354 concrete blocks in one minute
using elbow strikes (2004)

Bob Knight
3,014 wooden boards in 53 minutes
(2003)

Mike Reeves
415 wooden boards in one minute
(2002)

MORIHEI UESHIBA

Morihei Ueshiba was born in 1883. When he was young, he nearly died from scarlet fever. It left him a weak, feeble teenager.

Morihei Ueshiba

Ueshiba turned to jujutsu to regain his strength.

In the 1920s and 1930s, he developed a new martial art out of jujutsu. He called it aikido.

Aikido is mainly a system of self-defence. It uses an attacker's own energy to unbalance, disarm and throw the attacker.

Ueshiba was just 1.5 metres tall and weighed 50 kilograms, but he was a martial arts legend.

When he was 85, he gave an aikido demonstration.

Six young students attacked him at the same time. He sent his attackers flying with the smallest of movements.

Ueshiba in action

MUAY THAI LEGENDS

Muay Thai is Thai boxing. This martial art is at least 800 years old.

Muay Thai is like kickboxing except you can use your elbows and knees to strike. You can also grab hold of your opponent.

MUAY THAI LEGEND

Nai Khanom Tom was a warrior in Thailand. He was taken prisoner in a war between Thailand and Burma.

In 1774, he fought in Muay Thai bouts to gain his freedom. He beat 10 fighters from Burma in a row.

King Mangra of Burma was so impressed he gave him his freedom.

MODERN MUAY THAI LEGEND

Coban Lookchaomaesaitong is a modern Muay Thai legend. His nickname is "The Cruncher".

By the age of 15, Coban had fought over 35 times.

He won 250 out of 270 fights.

HADI SAEI

Hadi Saei is a taekwondo champion. He started practising martial arts when he was six years old.

Saei is the most successful sportsperson from Iran to enter the Olympics.

2008 – Saei wins gold at the Beijing Olympics

Year	Olympics	Saei's Medal
2008	Beijing	Gold
2004	Athens	Gold
2000	Sydney	Bronze

In 2003, an earthquake destroyed much of the city of Bam in Iran.

Saei sold his taekwondo medals at an auction to raise money for the victims.

aikido A Japanese martial art which uses holds and other moves to use an opponent's movement against them. Many people learn it as a method of self-defence.

bout A contest between two martial artists.

Burma A country in Asia. Today, it is called Myanmar.

death touch strike A type of secret move that can kill a person with just one touch of the hand. No one knows for sure if it really exists.

dislocate When a bone moves out of its socket.

intercept To stop or deflect.

Jeet Kune Do Martial arts invented by Bruce Lee. Martial artists use flowing movements, and stop an opponent's attacks with attacks of their own.

judoka A person who practises Judo.

jujutsu A Japanese martial art that uses throws and holds. Striking moves using tough parts of the body, such as the fists, are also used.

Kung Fu The name given to a group of martial arts that came from China.

legend A famous person who has become a hero to others.

opponent The person you are competing against.

Shaolin monk A monk (religious man) who follows the religion of Buddhism.

Triads Secret groups in China who are involved in crime.

MARTIAL ARTS WORDS

Martial arts may all be different but they share certain ways of behaving.

- **Accuracy** – You must perform your martial arts movements perfectly every time.

- **Discipline** – Keep control of your actions. Live and eat healthily.

- **Inner calm** – Learn to relax. Have your feelings under control at all times.

- **Practice** – Practise what you have been taught as often as you can.

- **Respect** – Always be polite and friendly to all teachers and other students.

- **Restraint** – Never use martial arts skills to attack.

MARTIAL ARTS ONLINE

Websites

http://www.wkausa.com

http://www.gichinfunakoshi.com

http://www.ijf.org/

http://www.wtf.org/